I0102223

THE **7** SECRETS OF

HIGH ACHIEVERS

Make Your Dream A Reality And

Become The Person You Are Destined To Be

AMOS AKINWALE

Publisher and author website and contact details:

www.amosakinwale.com

CONTENTS

WHY I WROTE THIS BOOK

A Long time ago, I made it one of my life's goals to equip myself with the skills needed to help people discover their dreams in life and become the best version of themselves.

There are 3 categories of people:

1. People who haven't a clue what they were born to do;

2. People who have a clue of what they were born to do but due to current circumstances have swept their dreams underneath the carpet, and;

3. People who are really sure of what they were born to do but just don't know how to make a head start on their dreams or need a

nudge or some practical guidance of the right steps to take along the way.

I was brought up in a single-parent home in a very rough area with little hope of success. As a result, I've been through a series of depression cycles along the way, including having suicidal thoughts when I didn't pass my University Entrance exam. However, I managed to pick myself up from the rut and God helped me turn my life around.

Today, I've successfully coached and mentored people out of their rut who have been way worse off than myself and who were also at the verge of giving up.

I also realise that there are people out there who just need someone who has been in their shoes to encourage and remind them that they are special, awesome, and unique.

In this book I've written, I'm here for YOU … to remind you that you are *very* much the above statement and so much more! No matter what you are going through, there is hope for you to get out of the rut, start fresh, and become the beautiful inspiration you are to the world.

WHY YOU SHOULD READ THIS BOOK

Like most people, I have often wondered what discovery of purpose truly means. How can I be fulfilled in life? How can I be more, do more, so that I can have more? There are books, magazines, articles, webinars, and resources out there that talk about how I can discover my purpose and achieve more. On Amazon alone, there are hundreds of thousands of books that refer to how people can know their life's purpose and achieve the dream in their hearts. That is a whole lot of material to explore!

The good news is you don't have to be confused anymore because this book will unveil the secrets you need to know and understand in order to become the best version of yourself. You will be empowered with keys to achieve better results and understand your purpose in a better light.

I will show you from different stories and experiences of self-made men and women how you, too, can create your own unique success code.

In this book, we will be exploring the secrets and proven principles of self-made millionaires and billionaires; including people who started with nothing, people who were college dropouts, people who didn't have the privilege to go to college, people who, at one time in their lives, could hardly afford a meal a day, and people who have been rejected by society, friends, family, and loved ones. These people, no matter how bad the situation was, did not give up and ended up making their dream a reality and becoming phenomenal icons who have inspired people and shaped history.

This book will help you get out of the ditch and rediscover yourself, but more importantly, make your dream a reality.

INTRODUCTION

"Some people dream of success,
while other people get up every morning
and make it happen."
– Wayne Huizenga

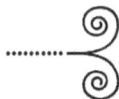

In 1890, a young preacher made an announcement in the newspapers that he was going to preach on a topic entitled, "What I would do if I had a million dollars!"

Philip D. Armour, who happened to be the rich packing-house king, saw this advertised announcement in the newspapers and became interested in it. During the sermon, the preacher painted a picture of a great school of technology where young people, regardless of financial circumstances, could be taught how to succeed in life by developing their ability to think practically rather than in theoretical terms. The preacher then said, "If I had a million dollars, I would start such a school."

Immediately after the end of the sermon, Philip Armour approached the young preacher and introduced himself. He told the preacher that he believed that what he said was possible and told the preacher to come down to his office the next morning to give him the one million dollars! This led to the birth of the Armour Institute of Technology with the young preacher as its first president. Today, the Armour Institute of Technology (now the Illinois Institute of

Technology), whose motto is "Transforming Lives. Inventing the Future," offers exceptional undergraduate and graduate degrees in various disciplines.

Before we start on this journey together, I would encourage you to go through this book at least once in order to fully *understand* the secrets in this book.

Buy an expensive journal of high value to you. Use this journal to capture the positive thoughts and ideas that come through your mind when reading this book. More importantly, use your journal to answer the questions in this book. These answers do not have to be perfect. However, there is power in writing down what comes to mind, especially the answers to the questions provided in this book.

Finally, allow me to tell you that your dream is possible, and you can become the best version of you! This book will help you achieve any dream you have ever wanted in life. As you learn about these key principles, be patient with yourself; it's a process that will lead to lasting change in your life. Knowing the secrets of high achievers will take you through the phases of character development that will eventually lead you to become the self-made high achiever who positively influences the world.

To your success!

Amos Akinwale

www.amosakinwale.com

Follow me on Instagram, Facebook, and Twitter @ amos365 for inspirational posts

CHAPTER ONE
DREAM:

High Achievers Have A Dream

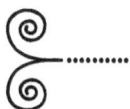

"I have a dream that one day, this nation will rise up and live out the true meaning of its creed; we hold these truths to be self-evident: that all men are created equal."
– Martin Luther King, Jr.

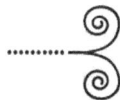

Every great person that has ever walked the face of the planet earth had a dream. Your dream is that idea that you can't let go of and that you are willing to give everything up for. Your dream is the reason why you exist. Every one of us exists for a reason, and the reason you exist is different from the reason others exist. When you find your reason for existence, it lights the passion within you. It ignites the fire that burns within you. It energizes you to take necessary action.

"Hold fast to dreams, for if dreams die, life is a broken-winged bird that cannot fly."
– Langston Hughes

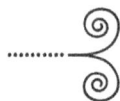

Most of the time when you look at where you are right now in your career, job, academics, finance, or relationships, and where you want to be in relation to your dream, you cannot compare the two. It seems as if it's far away. It looks as though it's laughable and unachievable. Nevertheless, you are not satisfied with where you are because your dream is calling you for more.

Martin Luther King Jr. said, *"I have a dream that my four little children will one day live in a nation where they will not be judged by the colour of their skin, but by the content of their character."*

We have seen the reality of Martin Luther King Jr.'s dream become possible on endless occasions; especially when Barack Obama defied the odds to become the first African American person (and I'm sure not the last), to become the President of the United States of America. However, at the time, his "I Have A Dream" public speech was delivered in Washington for Jobs and Freedom in 1963, this public statement would have been a source of ridicule for many Americans at the time. The reality is, a dream…

"It always seems impossible until it's done."
– Nelson Mandela

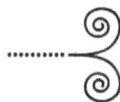

I believe that everyone (no one is exempt), has a dream that they have been created to pursue. However, while some are consciously aware of it, others are unconsciously aware that it exists. Nevertheless, the dream is there.

Your Dream …

1. *Gives You A Magnetic Pull.*

A dream is like a big magnet that pulls the greater version of you towards you. It draws you and gives you a drive. Your dream draws you constantly, and you are unable to let it go. The closer you are to your dream, the more fulfilled you become. The blueprint of your identity is hidden in your dream. It's that idea, that vision for your life that burns inside of you…something you can't ignore for long. It keeps bugging you; bubbling to the surface of your heart, and clamouring for your mind's attention.

2. You Are Willing To Give Up Everything For It

High achievers are willing to sacrifice their time, their money, and the so-called friends that don't believe in their dream, in order to achieve their dream. In other words, they are willing to do whatever it takes in order to make their dream a reality.

While others are busy partying and having fun, high achievers are busy thinking and strategizing about the next step to take towards achieving their dreams. While others are busy wasting away their lives, high achievers are busy planning their lives. This may lead to a life of loneliness for a while, but in the end, it is highly rewarding. According to the famous saying of a wise king in the book of Proverbs, "Wealth attracts many friends, but even the closest friend of the poor person deserts them!"

3. It Meets The Needs Of People

High achievers build their dreams on two pillars; Authenticity and People.

The first pillar is being true to who you are, your identity, your values, and your beliefs.

The second pillar is people, as you need people to achieve your dream.

*"From the womb that you came out from
to the tomb that you will end up in,
you will need people."*
– Amos Akinwale

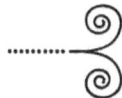

If God Himself thought people were worth dying for, then you cannot take people for granted. High achievers get all they want in life by helping enough people get what they want in life, as their dream is built on human need. Some of the questions you, therefore, need to ask yourself include:

- Will my dream help people?

- Will my dream improve the lives of people?

- Will my dream help reduce human suffering?

You cannot afford to look down on people because the person you see as a nobody today could be your golden key to your next level tomorrow. Your prosperity is not just for you; it's for others too. Your breakthrough is not just for you; it's for others too. Your dream is not just for you; it's for others too. Your dream is, therefore wrapped up in the dreams of others.

The Roadmap to Discovering Your Dreams

Below are a few questions I would strongly recommend you ponder deeply upon and answer in your journal:

1. Look Inward (Your Inner Reflection)

- What are your natural talents?

- What are your strengths?

- What do you love to do?

- What is really important to you?

- What are your top 5 values?

- If you were given a blank cheque to be and do something of value in the world and money was not an issue, what would it be?

Your inner desires are an important key to discovering your dream. Your dreams will make you desire and thirst for answers or solutions to something within. You can easily identify your dream by the desires that you have on the inside.

2. Look Outwards

- What do people say you are naturally good at doing?

- What issues are you easily drawn to?

  I like to summarise the second question in the following way:

  If you were watching TV or listening to a radio station, for instance, and an issue cropped up which caused you to get really angry about the issue or even moved you to tears, this is probably an indication that this so-called issue is linked to your desire to want to try and solve that issue and therefore linked to your dream.

- What do you have experience in?

  At times, we go through life without paying due attention to the *reasons why* we go through things, especially in tough times. Sometimes, your history or what you have been through in the past has a way of preparing you for what is ahead of you. In other words, the mess you've been in before in the past, or you find yourself in presently, can actually turn out to be your message to *inspire* others in the future.

CHAPTER TWO
VISUALISATION:

High Achievers Visualise Their Dream

"Visualization is the process of creating pictures in your mind of yourself enjoying what you want. When you visualize, you generate powerful thoughts and feelings of having it now. The law of attraction then returns that reality to you, just as you saw it in your mind."
– Rhonda Byrne

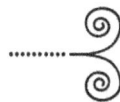

An important aspect of having a dream is visualising that dream. You must be able to see yourself fulfilling your dream long before it becomes a reality. When you visualise yourself accomplishing that dream, the law of attraction has a way of magnetising you in the direction of your dream.

In addition to visualisation, you must continuously profess positive affirmations, as what you say to yourself is powerful and can go a long way in shaping your destiny.

In a nutshell, an important way to summarise it is S^3

SEE: Visualise your dream

SAY: Profess positive affirmations; especially in spite of the discouraging current circumstances

SEE: Continue the above S's until you finally see your dream become a reality

See yourself succeeding in your presentation, your exams, your sales pitch, and in whatever you want to achieve.

A classic example of the visualisation and positivity process is seen in an interview by Oprah Winfrey with Jim Carey...

Jim Carey, the man famous for his lead role in the movie *The Mask*, made an unusual decision back in 1985. In 1985, he wrote himself a cheque for $10 million dated 10 years in the future for acting services rendered and kept it in his pocket...At that time he had nothing. He also had a habit of professing positive affirmations of what he desired to have...Again, at that time, he had nothing. Coincidentally, just before Thanksgiving in November 1995, Jim was cast in a movie, *Dumb and Dumber*... for that $10 million.

Despite the fact that you may have nothing at the moment or are living from paycheque to paycheque is not an indication that you'll end up with nothing. What matters is how you see yourself in the mirror.

Make it a daily habit to visualise yourself becoming the person you want to become every morning and before you go to bed at night.

If, for instance, you feel you don't have the confidence or what it takes to smash that interview or presentation, visualise yourself killing that presentation, people applauding you throughout your presentation, and even getting positive key referrals from your presentation.

Not only should you visualise yourself become that person and achieving the dream of acing your presentation, but also make it a habit to profess *specific* positive affirmations in the *present* tense. Look yourself in the mirror and tell yourself boldly and aloud when you wake or before you step out of the house, "I am the best at my presentation!"

When speaking positive affirmations, be mindful of the use of negative words in your sentences. For example, instead of saying, "I am *not* shy," a better approach would be, "I am bold." Other affirmations include, "I am wealthy," "Good things are happening for me," "I am loved so much," I am a masterpiece," "I am a genius," and so on.

Unfortunately, it is a norm for parents to use negative name words on their kids, even just casually. Terms such as "naughty little monster" are common phrases often used by parents, but then we wonder why the kids end up acting like the naughty little monster.

There is power in the use of your words, and what you say can either lift you up or tear you down.

Dr. Masaru Emoto, a Japanese scientist, experimented and explained in great depth the impact of our words. In a water experiment conducted by his team, they discovered that water exposed to loving words showed beautiful snowflake patterns. By contrast, they also discovered that water exposed to ill-mannered words showed disoriented patterns.

What is important to note from the above experiment is that our bodies consist of about 50 - 75% water, with babies and children having the highest percentage of water. It is, therefore, possible that the use of negative words does have a huge impact on that child.

The use of images displaying your ideal life and your dream around important areas of your home is a great way to aid your visualisation process. This is extremely powerful to serve as a constant reminder when the doubts come running through your head.

In addition, having a *Positive Affirmation* poster with *specific* positive affirmations linked to your dream images and around those images will help to reinforce your visualisation process consistently.

CHAPTER THREE
BELIEVE:

High Achievers Believe
Their Dream is Possible

*"The future belongs to those who believe
in the beauty of their dreams."*
– Eleanor Roosevelt

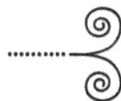

Even when the dream you have is crystal clear, you must undoubtedly believe that it is possible and that you are destined to achieve your wildest dreams. You must feel strong enough, smart enough, and capable enough to make your dream happen, despite your current circumstances.

As an individual, you must ensure you believe *strongly* in your dreams, as your belief will influence your behaviour, and your behaviour will ultimately determine what you become.

You must learn to eliminate conflicting situations, mindsets, limiting beliefs, and fears that are trying to sabotage you in achieving those dreams. You must learn to quiet the inner voice that keeps telling you or even laughing at you that it's impossible to achieve your dream.

"Whether you think you can, or you think you can't--you're right."
– Henry Ford

I am challenging you to be brave and be fearless. You must be fully persuaded about your dream and not live your life worrying about what people will say, especially when it sounds impossible at the time. The number 1 regret of the dying according to the book, *"The Top Five Regrets of the Dying,"* by **Bronnie Ware** is:

I wish I had the courage to live a life true to myself; not the life others expected of me!

"In order to succeed, we must first believe that we can."
– Nikos Kazantzakis

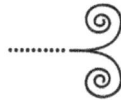

People give up easily on their dreams and on what they planned to achieve, and as a result, are unable to tap into their fullest potential because of the opinion of others about them. What their parents, ex-boyfriend, ex-girlfriend, friend, or partner said about them affected their will to believe and deflated their passion needed to follow through with their dream.

You must, however, never allow the opinions of others or current circumstances to define who you are, as you have the capacity to believe whatever you want to believe. You are the architect of your own belief and what you believe about yourself is entirely up to you.

*"If you believe in yourself and have
dedication and pride
– and never quit, you'll be a winner.
The price of victory is high, but so are the
rewards."*
– Paul Bryant

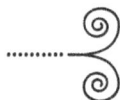

Moreover, you can either believe the facts, that is, what you can see physically around you, or the truth, which is what you can see with your heart (the truth about who you truly are that has not yet been revealed to the world). It's not what people think of you that counts, but what you believe about yourself that really matters.

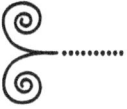

"Never allow the negative opinions of others become your reality."
– Amos Akinwale

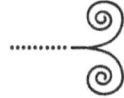

See the best in yourself, and you will be energized to eliminate limiting beliefs about yourself. If you don't know who you truly are, or you don't believe in yourself, it will be very difficult for someone else to believe in you. Even if you had a great idea, it would be very difficult for you to sell your idea successfully. Without belief in yourself, it will be very difficult to sell who you are authentically to the world.

Whether you are in pursuit of a job, a partnership opportunity, or at a networking event, you need to know that there's something of utmost value that you can offer and definitely bring to the table, no matter how inexperienced you may feel compared to the other party or competition.

You are different, you are special, you are awesome, you are unique, you are on an assignment, and you are here to solve a problem that only you have the answer to. You are here on purpose for a purpose, on a mission for a mission, and on assignment for an assignment. So stop comparing yourself with your colleague or competition and coming to the table from a beggar's position. Start to move into position from a person who can offer extreme value to the table!

"What you believe about yourself impacts your worldview, your self-worth, and your personality."
– Amos Akinwale

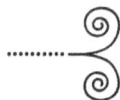

I have studied hundreds of books, and I discovered that high achievers faced pressures of doubt and criticism to give up on their dreams. However, they decided to choose the part of believing in themselves, their potential, and their inner power.

I've highlighted some great achievers below that defied the odds:

Albert Einstein, considered dyslexic, did not start to speak until the age of 3. Even still, he was not fluent and did not become fluent until the age of 9. He was described by his teacher as mentally slow, unsociable, and foolish. However, Albert Einstein believed in himself, went on to develop the theory of general relativity, and was regarded as the father of Modern Physics. He knew who he was and did not give up on his abilities.

Winston Churchill, the British World War II Prime Minister, failed his entrance exams twice to enter the British Royal Military College. He was also defeated in parliament but later went on to become the Prime Minister at the age of 62.

He said, *"Never give in, never, never, never, never, in nothing great or small, large or pretty, never give in except to convictions of honour and good sense."*

Richard Branson was also considered dyslexic and labelled as lazy and dumb by his teachers, dropped out of school at age 16, but went on to become the founder and chairman of one of the leading businesses in the world, the *Virgin Group*, as well as one of the most influential people in the world. He also owns an island and is in the process of sending people into outer space on holiday!

Talk about the opinions of others!

Anyone can say whatever they want to say about you; they are really entitled to their opinion. For high achievers, what is important to them is staying positive in the midst of opposition.

CHAPTER FOUR
DETERMINATION:

High Achievers have Rugged Determination

"Failure will never overtake me if my determination to succeed is strong enough."
— **Og Mandino**

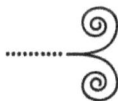

I have discovered that one of the secrets of highly successful people, the secret that separates the wealthy from the poor, an amateur from a champion, and an ordinary person from an extraordinary person is rugged determination.

The price of success is costly; however a rugged determination towards your dream will give you outstanding results if you are willing to pay the price of hard work towards your dream. Despite the obstacles surrounding you, a rugged determination to succeed will give you the strength to persevere.

This doesn't mean that success will happen for you if you are just determined to make it happen in a day or a week. It must become a habit, and you must be determined to achieve your dream…on a daily basis.

Also note that success is not achieved overnight, as it takes time and you must be willing to continue to press on regardless of the rejections and keep pushing yourself forward until you succeed…

Regardless of any challenges, you cannot afford to quit. No matter how difficult the challenge may seem, you must keep going. You must be determined if you want to make it. Remember, quitting means certain death for your goals; quitting means defeat, giving up, disappointment, and despondency. Don't deceive yourself into believing that you can quit "for a little while," or "until it gets easier," or "until you feel stronger." If you do this, you will effectively be starting from scratch again. If you can accept that, then go for it. If your dreams and goals are really important to you and are worth achieving, then be determined to absolutely give it all you have. The problem is that many of us give up even before we start to see results. Sadly, sometimes it occurs when the breakthrough is just around the corner.

"It's your rugged determination towards your dream that influences the outcome of your result in life."
– Amos Akinwale

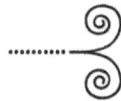

Your determination is an essential ingredient and presents as a strong motivator to achieving your success. You must be able to sustain your mental and physical toughness in order to achieve your desired dream. Wake up every day with the mindset and determination to work on something towards your goal of achieving your dream.

"Achieving Success is close to impossible if you are not determined."
– Amos Akinwale

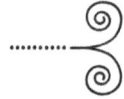

Success today was not obtained without effort; there is almost always a substantial amount of determination that occurred behind the scenes that led up to today's results. Sitting down will not produce success. Complaining will not help either. All you need to do is harness your strength, be determined, and just do it. As stressed by Walter D. Wintle in his poem below, "It's all in the state of mind":

Thinking

"If you think you are beaten, you are
If you think you dare not, you don't,
If you like to win, but you think you can't
It is almost certain you won't.

If you think you'll lose, you're lost
For out of the world we find,
Success begins with a fellow's will
It's all in the state of mind.

If you think you are outclassed, you are
You've got to think high to rise;
You've got to be sure of yourself before
You can ever win a prize.

Life's battles don't always go
To the stronger or faster man,
But sooner or later the man who wins
Is the man WHO THINKS HE CAN!"

A man or a woman that is determined are
people with vision, drive, motivation, aspiration,
and are not scared to put their best into what they
are passionate about.

How to Develop Determination

When writing down the answers in your journal, try to attach emotional importance to your reasons.

1. Write down 3 very compelling reasons why it is important for you to achieve your dream.

2. Write down 3 consequences of you not achieving your dream.

3. Write down the 3 most important categories of people who will be better off because you achieved your dream.

CHAPTER FIVE
FOCUS:

High Achievers are Extremely Focused

*"It's very tough for me to focus. I'm like:
'Look, something shiny! No, focus.
Oh, there goes a butterfly!'"*
– Gabby Douglas

Focus will energise you as a high achiever to limit your choices and focus on your focus. Clearly, if you want to be successful in less time and with less effort, focus is a skill you need to have. Focus is the ability to narrow your attention to a very specific point at any given time and follow-through.

Focus will empower you to follow through regarding things you plan to achieve, whether it's for your career, business, relationship, spiritual, family, financial, or emotional goals.

"The only reason men fail is because of broken focus."
– Mike Murdock

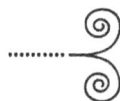

The Ability to Focus:

1. Empowers you to keep track of your goals.

2. Empowers you to help eliminate or minimise distractions.

3. Empowers you to have a crystal-clear perspective about your goal.

4. Empowers you to work efficiently and effectively.

5. Empowers you to be proactive and take productive steps.

6. Empowers you to avoid procrastination.

7. Empowers you to be motivated.

High achievers have a positive attitude and stay focused on positive things. They see challenges and obstacles as stepping stones to move forward towards their goal. Focus gives energy to the drive within; to the belief that their dream is not just going to happen someday, but that their dream is possible, and they deserve to have it. I love this poem by the **Sacred Poem** on Focus:

The light on the Horizon
The bull's-eye on the wall
The strength to do the impossible
When others simply fall

What creates the difference
Between those who succeed or fail

What creates a future
To which all other pale
Do you have the focus
To bring it all on view
To do what is required
That others fail to do

Thus, one course draws us forward
And brings success to light
It's there we meet our future
Magical and bright

If you are driving in a car and going in a particular direction, taking your hands off the steering wheel even for a second, could take you off course.

A great way to create focus is to create a to-do list as recommended by former U.S. President Dwight D. Eisenhower.

The Eisenhower's Principle separates tasks into one of 4 categories, the first category being the highest on your list of priorities and the fourth category being on your list of least priority:

1. DO NOW: Important and Urgent Task. E.g., Projects with a tight deadline

2. PLAN FOR: Important but not Urgent Task. E.g., Preparation towards your Dream

3. DELEGATE WHERE POSSIBLE: Not Important but Urgent Task. E.g., Some Emails and Calls

4. AVOID AT ALL COSTS: Not Important and Not Urgent Task. E.g., Timewasters

When focusing on your dream, it's also important to break your mega dream into easy and sizeable 'how to' achievable mini-goals and write them down in your journal. When you write your mini-goals to achieve your mega dream in your journal, your dream looks less complex and becomes easier to execute. Next, *plan* to take dedicated time to focus exclusively on one of your mini-goals.

CHAPTER SIX
PREPARATION:

High Achievers Prepare
for Their Dream

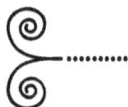

*"The dictionary is the only place that
success comes before work.
Hard work is the price we must pay for
success.
I think you can accomplish anything if
you're willing to pay the price."*
– Vince Lombardi

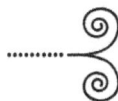

One of the key secrets of high achievers is the habit of preparing for the opportunity before it comes.

I remember the story of Susan Boyle, who became an international singer and a 3- time Guinness book of records holder. She was bullied as a child in school and nicknamed 'Susie Simple' because she was different from other children due to her learning disabilities – she was unable to get enough oxygen during her birth. This led to her dropping out of Edinburgh Acting School.

However, Susan believed in herself and kept pushing for the best. She saw herself at a very early age on a global platform. However, it took almost 35 years of her life to prepare for the dream she had. She recorded three tracks on a demo in 1998 and sent it to several radio talent competitions. However, it wasn't until 10 years later at *Britain's Got Talent*, that she had the opportunity to present what had taken her 35 years to prepare for in less than 4 minutes on a national stage. Fortunately, she wowed everyone! Nobody can forget the look on Simon Cowell's face when Susan began singing as he was left dumbfounded when Susan's tremendous voice. He was expecting to hear a terrible audition; however, her performance changed Simon's first impression of her.

"Believing is great; however, preparation for what you believe in is even better."

– Amos Akinwale

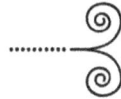

Preparing for an opportunity before it even appears, requires you to BE the person you want to be, even before the opportunity to become it arises, as there is power in the law of attraction. In other words, fake it until you make it.

High achievers don't wait for an opportunity to occur before they prepare, they create a door of preparation way before the opportunity knocks on that door. When the opportunity finally arrives at that door and collides with the preparation, success is inevitable. Some wait for the opportunity to come before they start to figure out what they want to do with the opportunity. High achievers, however, prepare themselves ahead of time by stretching themselves out of their comfort zone to learn new things and grow themselves with the required knowledge and skills to become an expert in the area, even when the opportunity has not yet arrived.

Price of Preparation + Right Opportunity
= Success

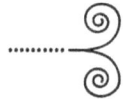

Achieving something of great value takes more than just a dream and belief. There are no shortcuts, no quick fixes, or an elevator to success. You must prepare to take the stairs. Having a grand dream is great – but when coupled with preparation, there is really no limit to what you can achieve. You just have to put in the effort. Seventy percent of people who win the lottery end up broke and bankrupt within 5-7 years because they are *not mentally prepared* to handle that kind of money.

"People with vision never stop preparing in advance."

– Amos Akinwale

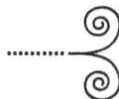

'Be Prepared Nuggets' for high achievers:

1. High achievers *envision* themselves achieving it long before it arrives on their door.

2. High achievers *prepare* in advance (mentally, emotionally, spiritually, and   physically) before the opportunity surfaces.

3. High achievers *never* stop learning new things.

Benefits of Preparation:

1. It helps you to know what you need to do and gets you ready for it.

2. It helps save time and resources.

3. It gives you the confidence about what you want and need to do.

4. It empowers you and fuels you to get ready to go forth and do what you believe in.

5. It helps drastically reduce the amount of stress you'd normally encounter if you were not prepared for the opportunity in advance.

6. It helps you deal with uncertainties and shortfalls that may occur, for example, in your project, presentation, or even in what to wear the next day.

Consequences of Lack of Preparation:

1. *It can cost you a life-time opportunity.*

2. *It can close doors against you.*

3. *It can lead to a lack of confidence.*

4. *It can bring anxiety, worry, frustration, stress, and disappointment.*

5. *It can lead to low or mediocre performance. An athlete or singer that is not   prepared, e.g., by proper eating and drinking or by not consistently training will not perform to their optimum level.*

CHAPTER SEVEN
CONSISTENCY:

High Achievers are Consistent

"When you look at people who are successful, you will find that they aren't the people who are motivated, but have consistency in their motivation."
– **Arsene Wenger**

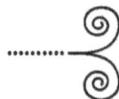

To be successful, you need to be consistent in what you do on a daily basis. You must regularly find 1% improvement in everything you always do and ask yourself, how can I do that 1% better than before? Consistency gives you the power to be focused and committed to your vision and goals. In order to be consistent, you must make up your mind to be committed to learning something new in relation to your dreams on a daily basis. Give a specific time to it and do it every day *regardless* of what happens.

Success is not cheap; it requires the continuous sacrifice of time. Preparation and consistency are essential ingredients whenever it comes to the achievement of success. The two work simultaneously in order to achieve outstanding results. The difference between high achievers and people who are not is the amount of *dedicated* and *quality time* invested in preparing for the opportunity ahead.

"Without hard work and discipline, it is difficult to be a top professional."
– Jahangir Khan

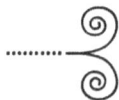

Inconsistency is the *silent* enemy of maximizing potential. True; it's hard to keep doing the same thing on a consistent basis. However, consistency is the most crucial aspect of training for high achievers. When high achievers pay the price of consistency, they become what people sitting on the sidelines perceive as overnight successes and a point of reference for these same people to emulate. Examples of consistency can be seen in the lives of sports figures; Boxers, Athletes, Gymnasts, Footballers, etc. Athletes have to train with consistency daily, have a consistent strict diet coupled with a regimented lifestyle. There is no high achiever that doesn't understand the law of consistency.

A professional athlete could take hours, days, weeks, months, or even years to perfect or just improve their game.

As Jesse Owens put it, *"A lifetime of training for just 100 seconds!"*

People perceived to be overnight successes by the general public are really just ordinary people who sacrificed a lot of their time to prepare for the opportunity ahead…*consistently.*

"You will always be consistent to what you attach importance to, and your results will clearly show it."
– Amos Akinwale

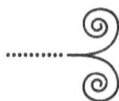

Benefits of Consistency:

1. **Consistency brings success and rewards:** when you are consistent to a vision, a calling, or a goal, you are rewarded for your hard work in following through to the end. There is no success without consistency, and people who are successful today are simply consistent people.

2. **Consistency brings expertise:** when you spend time learning whatever you need to learn in an area over and over again, in just a matter of time, you will become an authority in that area.

3. **Consistency brings continuity:** when you learn new things, you continually evolve in

your learning and development. In brutal terms, it's either you are growing your mind or killing it.

4. **Consistency brings stability:** you become stable and not moved by the opinion of others.

5. **Consistency brings orderliness and reliability:** you become very reliable to work with.

6. **Consistency makes people responsible and dependable:** it portrays and magnifies you in front of people as someone of good character and values.

7. **Consistency empowers:** you are empowered to finish what you have started… well.

Hindrances to consistency:

1. **Discouragement:** when things don't happen according to plan.

2. **Delay:** when the product or result you expect is delayed.

3. **Loss:** experiencing loss in business, career, or life.

4. **Disappointment**: when people or partners you trust refuse to back you up after they have promised to help you.

5. **Lack of discipline:** when you spend all the time you are supposed to invest in your life and dreams in front of the TV watching Netflix or immersed in social media, more importantly, time wasters.

Consequently, inconsistency can lead to discouragement, abortion of dreams, and lack of progress. What you do on a daily basis must be consistent in order to make it work.

I'll tell you a story of a friend of mine that shared with me his dream of losing weight. He was determined in his mind to lose weight and started watching his calorie intake. However, two days later, he went back to his old habits; he would drink about 4 cans of fizzy drinks and 4 chocolate bars. He was also living on fast food almost every day. The last time I checked, he hasn't really lost any weight. If you want to be a high achiever and you are not consistent, it is very difficult for your dream to become a reality.

If you took your hands off the steering wheel of a ship going toward a destination, after a while the ship will drift off in another direction.

I love this poem by **Selby Evergreen**:

Consistency is still a virtue

And so I'll hold it close

Despite all those who say it's needless,

Who say that none of those

Men of greatness needed it

Or wanted it at all

They say that men of greatness did

By this consistency fall

On the part of those who mocked them,

Consistent in their hate

But those great men themselves they were

Consistently so great

And never stopped along their tracks,

Did never stop nor pause

And credit inconsistency,

It's truly not the cause

Of greatness, friendship, faithfulness,

It's faithless cheaters' word

To laud the perks of randomness

Is really quite absurd

And even more, this comes from me,

A person inconsistent,

But are we all, or are we ever,

Truly that consistent?

Make up your mind now to work consistently towards your goals, and you will definitely achieve your dream.

CHAPTER EIGHT
HABITS OF HIGH ACHIEVERS

"The secret of success is hidden in your daily routine."
– John C. Maxwell

1. **Stand for what you believe in.**

"A man who won't die for something is not fit to live."
– Martin Luther King, Jr.

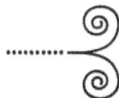

This can be very easy for some people, however not for everyone. Standing up for what you believe in, especially when all odds are against you is considered as one of the strongest qualities of high achievers. The vast majority of people in our society choose to keep quiet, stay obscured in the crowd, lose their voice, and their *authentic* self. However, we are liberated, and we are in charge of what we want in life, not what others want for us.

2. Stand up for someone who can't do it on their own.

There are people all around you right now who aren't decision-makers, who don't have a voice, and who don't know how to speak up. So, to speak up and give a voice to the voiceless or a group of people without a voice is something that every high achiever does. They are a reference point of light that help others to shine.

Marianne Williamson rightly put it in her poem:

> *Our deepest fear is not that we are*
> *inadequate.*
> *Our deepest fear is that we are powerful*
> *beyond measure.*

*It is our light, not our darkness that most
frightens us.
Your playing small does not serve the world.
There is nothing enlightened about
shrinking
so that other people won't feel insecure
around you.
We are all meant to shine as children do.
It's not just in some of us; it is in everyone.
And as we let our own lights shine,
we unconsciously give other people
permission to do the same.
As we are liberated from our own fear,
our presence automatically liberates others.*

3.   Give someone a second chance.

It's easy to give up on people, especially when they are not doing very well. When someone fails, it's easy to find a replacement for them or someone else to do the job. Successful people have failed on several occasions but were given the opportunity to learn from their failures, become better, and grow. Learning from past mistakes can be the greatest teacher, but if we don't give people the opportunity to fail before criticizing them, then we are not embracing the habits of high achievers.

As **A.P.J. Abdul Kalam** once said, "*If you fail, never give up because F.A.I.L. means, "First Attempt In Learning."*

High Achievers have a high degree of Physical Intelligence (PQ), Intellectual Intelligence (IQ), Emotional Intelligence (EQ), and Spiritual Intelligence (SQ).

The four are interrelated and play a key role in achieving success.

1. PQ

High Achievers are able to listen to internal messages communicated by their body and respond effectively to those messages. In identifying their wants versus their needs; e.g. knowing when enough is enough when eating, eating the right kinds of foods, or knowing when there is a need to work out despite feeling lazy, they are able to keep their body in check by living a healthy lifestyle necessary for the body's physiological functions to work appropriately.

2. IQ

High Achievers are always on the lookout for new information in order to improve themselves and perfect their skill. High achievers are consistent when embarking on a life-long journey of continuing education to improve their IQ. They are also always conscious of the network of people they surround themselves with, ensuring that the network of people are positive-minded people. They will always be involved in organisations where their work culture engages in and embraces life-long learning.

Their motto is:

"The day you stop learning is the day your brain starts dying," in other words, YOU.

3. EQ

High achievers always feel the need to give something back to society. They are socially empathetic and are service-oriented. Bill Gates, who dedicates his life to philanthropy, is a classic example of a man who lives by service to mankind.

They are also self-aware; able to manage self, and their emotions as well as stay calm and in control when under pressure; especially when things don't go according to plan or dealing with uncertainties or very difficult people. They realise that one bad reaction to an incident can lead to a chain of devastating and sometimes irreversible consequences that could have easily been avoided had they kept their emotions in check.

High achievers have mastered the art of quieting the tiny inner voices; the saboteurs that say they are not good enough or cannot make it. They are mindful of the use of their body language and *how* they communicate when actively engaging with all manners of people and different personality types. They are also mindful of their body language when in a rest state, as they realise that their body language plays a crucial part in their countenance and emotional state.

4. SQ

Lastly, high achievers have a deep understanding of who they are, their worldview, as well as an awareness of the worldview of others. They understand their values, their purpose in life, and their vision, and are able to act with wisdom and compassion.

They are able to visualise their desired future in the present effectively. This last one requires consistent thoughtful meditation and faith to visualise the images of their desired life that are not yet in existence. In the visualisation chapter mentioned previously, I spoke of the ability to envision yourself winning that presentation with the audience clapping long before you step onto the podium. Successful athletes are often able to use this technique effectively when they visualise their action of winning the race or the game long before the day of actual performance. They do not allow for negative thoughts to find a place to hide in their conscious or subconscious mind. They are continually renewing their mind daily with positive thoughts and have a journal where they write down their desired lifestyle as though they are already living in that moment.

10 Positive Mindsets of High Achievers

1. *Love Yourself*
   You kickstart a process of miracles when you begin to love yourself.

2. *Value Your Own Idea*
   Your idea is your signature to the world – value it.

3. *Build Your Confidence*
   When you build your confidence, you become a force to be reckoned with.

4. *Think Positive*

   Your life goes in the direction of your thoughts.

5. *Eliminate Limiting Beliefs*

   You have no limits…except for the ones you place on yourself.

6. *Learn To Accept Compliments*

   Compliments are part of your confidence building blocks.

7. *Admire Your Strengths*

   Whatever you don't admire cannot add value to you.

8. *Always Improve Yourself*

   Keep growing, keep evolving, because there is greatness within you.

9. *Set Goals And Hit Them*

   With goals, we create the future in advance.

10. *Tell Yourself Good Things Daily*

   What you tell yourself daily will either lift you up or tear you down.

CHAPTER NINE
SHORT STORIES OF HIGH
ACHIEVERS:

Self-made Men and Women who Became Millionaires and Billionaires.

"Success is no accident. It is hard work, perseverance, learning, studying, sacrifice, and most of all, love of what you are doing or learning to do."
– Pele

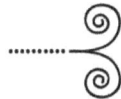

It doesn't matter who you are, how old you are, and where you are coming from, or what your area your dream is in. If you pursue your dream whole-heartedly and follow the principles of successful people, you will end up becoming a self-made inspiration to the world.

Below is a list of a few self-made men and women who started encountering a number of hurdles in their daily life, but found a way to transform their lives. As of 2019, all self-made men and women mentioned below have a net worth of at least $1 million today.

COLONEL SANDERS

His father died when he was just 5 years old. He quit school at age 16. He had lost 4 jobs by age 17. He failed in other careers throughout his life, including being a lawyer and salesman.

He retired at the age of 65 and decided to commit suicide. He sat down writing his will, but instead, he wrote what he would have accomplished with his life and about how good of a cook he was.

He then borrowed $87.00 and fried some chicken using his *secret* recipe, went door-to-door to sell them and was rejected 1,009 times from restaurants where he wanted to license his recipe.

Fortunately, the 1,010th restaurant gave him a yes, and Kentucky Fried Chicken (KFC) was born.

At the time of his death in 1980, Colonel Sanders had an estimated net worth of $3.5 million. As of 2019, KFC has a net worth of $8.5 billion and has over 22,000 outlets in 135 countries.

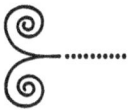

"If you get No as an answer, remember N.O. means 'Next Opportunity'."
– A.P.J. Abdul Kalam

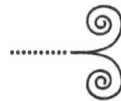

OPRAH WINFREY

Oprah was born from a very poor background. Her parents, unmarried at the time of her birth, soon separated after she was born, and was left under the care of her maternal grandmother on the farm. Oprah was so poor as a child that she wore a dress made of potato sacks.

She then went on to live with her mother from the age of 6 in a very poor and dangerous neighbourhood. Oprah had a very troubled childhood with years of repeated sexual abuse starting at the age of 9 from male relatives and friends of the family. At age13, she ran away from home and became pregnant at the age of 14 with a son who died within 2 weeks of birth.

She was sent to live with her father and under his strict parental guidance, redirected herself on the right path towards success.

She went on to become the first black female billionaire and now has her own television network, OWN.

As of 2019, she has an estimated net worth of $2.7 billion.

SHAHID KHAN

He relocated to the United States from Pakistan to study Engineering at the University of Illinois with $500 to his name. He washed dishes in restaurants for $1.20 an hour while attending the University of Illinois in order to pay for his expenses.

He went on to work for Flex-N-Gate before leaving to start his own company, Bumper Works. However, he was soon sued shortly afterward by Flex-N-Gate who claimed he stole trade secrets. Unable to pay a decent lawyer to defend his case, Shahid buried himself in the law library and went on to effectively defend his company. Shahid eventually went on to buy his former employer Flex-N-Gate.

He is now the sole owner and CEO of Flex-N-Gate, one of the largest private companies in the U.S. He bought the NFL's Jacksonville Jaguars. becoming the first ethnic minority owner in the history of the NFL and also bought Premier League Soccer Club Fulham.

As of 2019, he has a net worth of $8.1 billion.

DENZEL WASHINGTON

He was born to Denzel Sr., a Pentecostal minister, and his wife, a beautician and gospel singer. He first took the stage around the age of seven in a talent show at his local Boys & Girls Club.

When he was 14-years-old, his parents were divorced, and he became involved with street violence. His mother had to send him away to boarding school to help discipline him. He went to Fordham University and graduated with a B.A. in Drama and Journalism in 1977.

He went on to pursue acting as a career and within a short span of time began to receive national attention for his work on the television drama, *St. Elsewhere*. Today he is an actor, producer, and director who has received two Golden Globe awards, one Tony Award, and two Academy Awards.

As of 2019, he has a net worth of approximately $220 million.

ELON MUSK

Elon was an immigrant from South Africa. At age 10, his parents got divorced. He was bullied until the age of 15 before learning how to defend himself through karate and wrestling.

At the age of just 12, he created a space-themed PC game called *Blaster* and sold it to a computer magazine for $500.

He launched his first company with his brother; Zip2, after dropping out of Stanford University just 2 days after enrolling to do a Ph.D. in Energy Physics.

He then wanted a safe payment method, so he created X.com in 1999 (later becoming PayPal).

He wanted to go to space, so he created his third company; SpaceX in 2002 at the age of 30.

He wanted to drive an electric car, so he co-founded Tesla Motors in 2003.

He wanted faster transportation, so he developed Hyperloop.

He became a multi-millionaire in his late twenties, and as of 2019 has a net worth of $20.2 billion.

TATYANA BAKALCHUK

While on maternity leave with her infant son, both her and her husband, Vladislav struggled to make ends meet for their son. She also thought about the difficulties young mothers encountered when trying to shop for clothes and care for their new-born.

Tatyana, therefore, decided to start an online store while on maternity leave in her apartment to bring in an extra flow of cash and solve the problem. She was fond of bright colours so she called her online company *Wildberries*. She was also the company's first customer.

Wildberries became the first online superstore in Russia and today is one of the most valuable companies on the Russian internet, selling over $1.9 billion worth of apparel in 2018.

As of 2019 Tatyana, now the mother of four and sole owner of her business has as estimated net worth of $1 billion.

STEVE JOBS

Steve was born to university students, Abdul Jandali and Joanne Schieble, who were unmarried at the time. They gave him up for adoption as their parents objected to their relationship. Steve struggled with formal education, and teachers reported that he was a handful to teach. After just six months at college, Jobs quit but continued to pop in on Calligraphy courses while staying in his friend's dorm room.

In 1976, Steve co-founded the Apple Computer Company in his garage, which at the time specialised in selling circuit boards.

In 1983, Steve was ousted from the board and stripped of all power and control. Steve, therefore, had to sell his shares and resign in 1985.

He went on to create NeXT, which became unsuccessful at first in selling hardware but then became successful at selling software, which Apple eventually bought as an act of desperation in 1996, bringing Steve back to Apple as the new chief executive.

He went on to transform the ailing Apple into one of the world's most well-known names in computers and attributes his time spent in calligraphy classes as being instrumental to his designs for Apple's multiple typefaces.

He was also the owner and CEO of Pixar films; famous for producing *Toy Story*, which was later sold to Disney in 2006 at $7.4 billion making him the largest shareholder in Disney.

He had a net worth of $7 Billion before he died in 2011.

KIRAN MAZUMDAR-SHAW

Kiran was born in Bangalore, India.

Kiran aspired to become a medical doctor while growing up but did not obtain a scholarship to go to medical school. Her father at the time encouraged her to become a Brewmaster, which at the time was a male-dominated industry and non-traditional for a woman to embark upon.

Kiran embarked on the unknown journey with the faith and belief of her father. She moved to Australia to study Malting and Brewing in Federation University. She was the only girl in her class, but she went on to top the class and graduated as a Master Brewer.

Seeing there was no future working as a female Master Brewer in India, Kiran decided to work for a couple of years in Australia. She then switched her job to work for a Biopharmaceutical company, *Biocon Biochemical Limited*, in Ireland before making the bold move to return home to India and set up her own branch, *Biocon India*.

Funding at the time was a big issue for young Kiran at the time. She also struggled to get employees to work for her start-up. Her gender was a major hurdle to both issues.

However, she didn't get discouraged by the lack of support. Instead, she worked hard with what she had to build her biotechnology company, which is now India's largest biopharmaceutical company and making her the wealthiest woman in her country.

As of 2019, she has a net worth of $2.4 billion.

ROMAN ABRAMOVICH

He lost his parents soon after he was born at the early age of 2. As an orphan, he was looked after by his paternal uncle and spent his childhood in the desolate region of the Komi Republic in Northern Russia.

Roman went through a tough childhood and soon understood the value of money, learning how to save while a student. This helped him begin his first venture of plastic toy, making selling plastic ducks.

He dropped out of two colleges and also left the army out of boredom, realizing the army wasn't his dream. He decided to pursue his passion and went on to pursue a number of business ventures in oil and real estate.

He now has the world's largest yacht, a Boeing 767, is the proud owner of the Chelsea Football Club, and ranks on the list of one of the richest people in the world.

As of 2019, he has a net worth of $12.4 billion.

BILL GATES

Bill Gates went to Harvard College for two years. At college, he spent most of his time on computers with little interest in studying other subjects. He, therefore, dropped out of Harvard in order to pursue his passion and co-founded Microsoft.

In 2008, he left his daily job at Microsoft to dedicate and focus more on Philanthropy, including global issues ignored by the government as well as help improve standards of public school education in the United States. He finally stepped down as chairman in 2014.

He has been described as the most successful Harvard dropout, consistently topping Forbes's list as the worlds' wealthiest person on the planet.

His net worth as of 2019 is currently at approximately $105.6 billion.

THOMAS EDISON

He did not learn to talk until he was almost four years old. When he was 7 years old in 1854, he attended school for only twelve weeks. While attending school, he was easily distracted and hyperactive. He was withdrawn from school by his mother as his teacher couldn't manage him, and his mother home-schooled until he was eleven years of age. He was selling newspapers at the age of thirteen, and after a while, he then decided to publish his own newspaper brand.

Moreover, Edison, following his passion for science, set up a mini-laboratory in a baggage car. While he was experimenting one day, the car caught fire and was forced to sell newspapers again as a result of that incident.

He went on to invent the world's first practical incandescent light. During the experiment leading up to the success story, he had failed to make the light bulb work 10,000 times! However, he didn't see himself as a failure; as he quoted in his now-famous quote, "*I have not failed. I've just found 10,000 ways that won't work.*" Eventually, it took him over a year to get a working light bulb that burned for 13.5 hours. He also developed the first electric power generation and distribution system that would supply electricity to homes in the region where he lived.

He had a net worth of $12 million at the time of his death in 1931.

GEORGE CLOONEY

George developed Bell's Palsy while he was in middle school, which partially paralysed his face. As a result, he was nicknamed Frankenstein. Even though he eventually overcame the condition, it had a lasting effect on him. He dropped out of college and worked odd jobs, including selling shoes. He even tried out for a baseball team; the Cincinnati Reds, but didn't win a contract.

His cousin eventually got him a small part to play in a feature film. He took bit parts on TV shows before getting his big break.

He is now a superstar, receiving 8 Academy Award nominations and winning 2 Oscars.

As of 2019, he has a net worth of approximately $500 million making him one of the most highly sought actors in Hollywood and richest actors in the world.

BARACK OBAMA

Barack's parents divorced when he was just 2-years-old. As a child, he did not have a relationship with his father and therefore struggled. He only saw him once more after his parents had divorced when his father made a brief visit to Hawaii in 1971.

Ten years later, his father tragically lost both his legs in a serious car accident which confined him to a wheelchair. He soon lost his job afterward. The next year, he was involved in yet another serious car accident. This time he lost his life. Barack was 21-years-old at the time, and this had a devasting impact on Barack. As a teenager, he used alcohol and drugs, including marijuana and cocaine. He constantly struggled with his identity and was conscious of his African-American heritage.

Eventually, Obama paid an emotional visit to the graves of his father and paternal grandfather in Kenya.

Returning from Kenya with a sense of renewal, he enrolled into Harvard Law School and went on to defy all odds by becoming:

The first African American President of the prestigious Harvard Law Review in 1991.

The third African American to serve in the U.S. Senate in 2005, and

The 44th President, but yet again the first African American President…this time of the United States of America in 2009. As of 2019, he has a net worth of $40 million.

HENRY FORD

Shortly after his mother died, Henry decided to leave his family home at age 16 to get a job. Years later, he was hired as an engineer by the Edison Illuminating Company, where he worked his way up in a short space of time to become Senior Engineer.

He later founded 2 companies, but unfortunately, each company filed for bankruptcy. The first was Detroit Automobile Company; the second was the Henry Ford Company.

However, he later found success on his third attempt when he founded the Ford Motor Company. This company went on to transform the face of the automobile industry, selling millions of vehicles during his lifetime.

By the 1940s, Henry rose to become the wealthiest man on the planet. Upon his death in 1947, Henry Ford was worth the equivalent of approximately $200 billion today.

INGVAR KAMPRAD

He was a village boy from a farm in the rural area of Sweden. He was dyslexic, which made it difficult for him to get good grades at school. He began his career selling Christmas decorations and matches at the age of 6. At the age of 10, he began to sell Christmas decorations, fish, and pencils.

At age 17, his father rewarded him with a small monetary amount for doing well in school despite being dyslexic. He used the money to start a furniture merchandise store. His vision was to design a product that was affordable, modern, and simple. He proceeded to become the founder of IKEA. However, due to the incredibly low prices, manufacturers began protesting against IKEA, forcing him to design items in-house. He went on to innovate the flat-pack idea, making furniture affordable for customers.

IKEA is currently the world's largest furniture retailer in the 21st century, with 423 stores operating in 52 countries (at the time of this writing).

He had an estimated net worth of $58.7 billion before he died at age 91.

MICHEAL JORDAN

He was once cut out from the high school varsity basketball team as a sophomore. This inspired him to work harder and get better and eventually made the team, leading them to the State Championship.

He dropped out of university and was chosen to be on the *Chicago Bulls*, which was not one of the best NBA teams and was a losing team at the time.

Michael put his heart into it and changed the fate of the team, and the Chicago Bulls started winning most of their games.

He ended up becoming the wealthiest NBA player; the only billionaire athlete in history, and greatest basketball player ever with records of receiving 6 NBA championships, 5 NBA most valuable player awards, and 14 NBA All-Star appearances.

As of 2019, Michael has a net worth of $1.9 billion.

J.K. ROWLING

J.K. Rowling had always wanted to be a writer. At the age of 6, she wrote her first book, although little came from her early efforts. She was teased at school because of her name, with people calling her 'rolling pin.'

She didn't particularly have a great teenage life, as her mother, who battled with Multiple Sclerosis at the time, took a toll on the family. She studied French at university from the advice her parents offered. However, she regretted studying it, admitting that English would have been a better option.

It was in 1990 on an over 4-hour delay journey from Manchester to London that she first conceived the idea of Harry Potter and began to form the characters of the series. When she got back to her flat in London, she immediately began to write her new book. Unfortunately, later that year, when J.K. Rowling was 25 years old, her mother finally died, succumbing to her disease. This had a traumatizing effect on her.

She started dating a man and became pregnant. However, she later miscarried. They eventually got married and had a daughter, but it was a very shaky marriage, and they divorced after about 13 months.

Living in a tiny apartment, jobless, a single mother, and penniless in Britain, J.K. Rowling became very depressed, having suicidal thoughts. She lived on state benefits and spent most of her spare time writing the Harry Potter series when her daughter was sleeping next to her.

When she eventually finished her book, she sent her manuscript to many traditional publishers where she received numerous rejections and was advised to get a 9-to-5 job. She eventually got the green light from a small publisher at the time, Bloomsbury, in 1997 to publish the first book of the Harry Potter series.

As of 2019, her books have consistently topped the best-sellers list, she is the highest-paid author, and has an estimated net worth of $92 million.

LEONARDO DEL VECCHIO

Born to a very poor family, he was forced to live in an orphanage at age 7 under the care of nuns because his widowed mother could not afford to support her 5 children.

He worked as an apprentice at a car and eyewear parts factory at age 14 to support his impoverished family and put himself through design school. He also threw himself into learning *everything* there was to learn about the eyeglass industry from the design to the marketing.

At age 25, he founded Luxottica. In 2018, Luxottica merged with Essilor, becoming the largest producer and retailer of sunglasses and prescription glasses in the world.

As of 2019, he has an estimated net worth of $23.2 billion.

RALPH LAUREN

He was a son of Jewish immigrants who lived in poverty in the states. He was teased when he was in his late teens because of his name, Lipschitz before he changed it to Lauren.

When Ralph was in high college, he wrote "millionaire" as one of his life's goals. He was a drop out from Baruch College. He went to college to study business and couldn't continue after the second year. He then joined the army and served there for two years.

He had no formal education or training in fashion but an ambition to succeed and a passion for designing clothes. He became a clerk for Brooks Brothers before going on to open his own colourful necktie store, which he branded Polo. He sold $500,000 worth of ties in the first year.

He is now a fashion icon and as of 2019, has an estimated net worth of $6.5 billion.

WARREN BUFFETT

As a child, he got horrible grades and even ran away from home.

He bought 6 shares of Cities Services (3 of these shares were for his older sister) at $38 and sold them at $40 when he was just 11-years-old.

He had already made $5,000 (equivalent to $42,610.81 in 2000) from delivering newspapers when he was just 17-years-old.

He was rejected for admission by Harvard Business School. His initial investments in Texaco and some real estates were also a failure.

He is now one of the most successful investors of all time and one of the most respected businessmen in the world today. As of 2019, he has a net worth of $84.3 billion.

ZHOU QUNFEI

Zhou lived in extreme poverty, not knowing where her next meal would come from. Her father went blind and lost a finger in a factory accident just before she was born. Her mother died at the early age of 5. At age 16, she dropped out of high school to work as an assembly worker in a watch lens factory. She took herself to night school and always *dreamed* of starting a business. She worked *towards* saving about $2,500 to start up her first company – a family lens watch workshop and over the next decade *built* a factory making watch lenses and employing 1,000 people.

However, a business rival was jealous and teamed up with the raw material supplier to try and get her out of the game. She became suicidal and was just about to commit suicide when she got a phone call from her daughter who pulled her back and made her remember the reason why she got into the business in the first place. She couldn't give up on her family or employees. She had to *press on*.

Today, Zhou is known as the world's richest self-made woman according to Forbes, and as of 2019 has an estimated net worth of $4.6 billion. Her company *Lens Technology* is a smartphone screen supplier, whose customers include Samsung, LG, Microsoft, Nokia, and Tesla.

She attributes *Perseverance* as a vital key to her success.

TRAVIS KALANICK

Kalanick was bullied by older kids when growing up. He vowed that never again would he be pushed around. He went to UCLA to study electrical engineering but dropped out to start a company alongside several of his classmates; *Scour Inc.*, a peer-to-peer search engine, which was eventually sued for a quarter of a trillion dollars for copyright infringement by several entertainment companies before filing for bankruptcy.

He rebounded from bankruptcy by wooing investors to start up his next company; *Red Swoosh*, a networking software company. He eventually sold the company for nearly $23 million and became an angel investor for promising start-ups.

Kalanick's distaste of taxis originated from his own bad experience using them and in 2009, he co-founded *Uber*, which is now a worldwide phenomenon in driving services.

As of 2019, he has a net worth of $3.4 billion.

KELVIN PLANK

Frustrated with his sports cotton t-shirts always soaked in sweat, he was pretty much broke when he maxed out his finances to start his T-shirt business.

He worked from his grandmother's basement for nearly 2 years, exaggerating to early customers and making them have a perception that his company, *Under Armour*, was a big company.

Today, *Under Armour* employs over 11,000 people and as of 2019 has an estimated net worth of $1.8 billion.

JACK MA

He was born in Hangzhou, China, and was very poor when growing up. He sat for a university admission examination and failed. Twice. On his third attempt, he got admitted and graduated with a degree in English. He was looking for a job and was rejected more than a dozen times, including one at Kentucky Fried Chicken. He eventually got a job as an English teacher though he was paid only $12 a month.

He visited the United States in 1995 where he saw the internet and his first computer for the very first time. He recognised a huge gap and started China pages where Chinese content was put online. He started a Chinese online directory, and it failed.

He later started Alibaba in 1999 with a group of friends, which became a huge success.

He became the wealthiest self-made man in China and as of 2019 has an estimated net worth of $38.7 billion.

CHAPTER TEN
A FINAL NOTE

In addition to all of the above, there are 2 things I want to leave you with:

1. **Write Your Vision:** The first is writing and documenting your dream and the reasons *why* it is important for you to achieve your dream in your journal. There is extreme power in documenting your ideas and putting it into plain writing so that you may always revisit the reasons why you embarked on your journey of success in the first place, and encourage yourself to press on and not give up along the way.

2. **The God Factor:** The second but most powerful of all is the God factor. On your journey to achieving success, develop an

awareness about God. Seek to know Him. Make it a priority to put God first in all your decisions, especially when you are confused (no matter how small), and He will surely direct your paths. If you consult with God and ask for His guidance, He will undoubtedly elevate you and provide you with the strength you need to carry on in difficult times.

Finally, I believe there is a dream on the inside of you. You are not a mistake; you are not a failure; you are not what your past says. You, too, can go after your wildest dreams! Never allow your past to determine what your future should look like. You have what it takes. You are a world changer and the world's waiting for you just to *show up*. All the high achievers mentioned in this book and in the world today are humans, just like you. However, they refused to be labelled by their limitations. They had a dream, strongly believed in their dream, and as a result, made adequate preparations towards their dream with a strong determination to succeed. This made them extremely focused and consistent in making their dreams a reality. If they can do it, so can you.

These people decided that they didn't want to be just mere men and women on the sidelines, waiting for things to happen or watching things happen. However, these people decided that they wanted to be a part of the making of history by becoming self-made men and women; the high achievers who are currently still busy shaping history today!

ABOUT THE AUTHOR

Amos has a background in Research and Development, Analytical Chemistry, Neuro-Linguistics Programming, Coaching, and Project Management. He studied at Cambridge University, is a Member of Association for Coaching, and he is the Youth Pastor at City of David, Cambridge, where he helps teenagers, students, and young working professionals to identify their gifts and maximise their potential. As a coach, mentor, and inspirational speaker, he has a passion to make a difference in the lives of people. He has received recognition awards from past Mayors of Cambridge for his impact and contribution to helping young people discover their leadership potential.

NOTES:

www.ingramcontent.com/pod-product-compliance
Lightning Source LLC
Chambersburg PA
CBHW022120280326
41933CB00007B/470